Popcorn

Out and About

Honor Head

WAYLAND

Explore the world with **Popcorn** - your complete first non-fiction library.

Look out for more titles in the **Popcorn** range. All books have the same format of simple text and striking images. Text is carefully matched to the pictures to help readers to identify and understand key vocabulary.
www.waylandbooks.co.uk/popcorn

Published in 2013 by Wayland
Copyright © Wayland 2013

Wayland
338 Euston Road
London NW1 3BH

Wayland Australia
Level 17/207 Kent Street
Sydney NSW 2000

Editor: Jean Coppendale
Designer: Alix Wood
Picture research: Taglines Creative Limited

British Library Cataloguing in Publication Data:
Head, Honor
    Out and about. - (Popcorn. Watch out!)
    1. Accidents - Prevention - Juvenile literature
    I. Title II. Series III. Out and about
    363.1-dc22

ISBN 978 0 7502 7818 8

10 9 8 7 6 5 4 3 2 1

Printed and bound in China
Wayland is a division of Hachette Children's Books, an Hachette UK Company.
www.hachette.co.uk

Photographs:
Cover, 4 Maxim Slugin/Shutterstock; 5 Craig Lovell Eagle Visions Photography/ Alamy; 6 Monkey Business Images/Shutterstock; 7 Shutterstock; 8 Jacek Chabraszewski/ Shutterstock; 9 Hallgerd/Shutterstock; 10 JUPITERIMAGES/Polka Dot/Alamy; 11 Elena Elisseera/Shutterstock; 12 Anna Karwowska/Shutterstock; 13 Dinodia Images/Alamy; 14 Altrendo Images/Getty; 15 Digital Vision/Alamy; 16 Elmtree Images/ Alamy; 17 Peter Titmuss/Alamy; 18 Jacek Chabraszewski/Shutterstock; 19 Chrislofoto/ Shutterstock; 20 Photolocation3/Alamy; 21 Morgan Lane Photography/Shutterstock.

Contents

Going out 4

At the shops 6

Let's play 8

At the park 10

The playground 12

School time 14

Train safety 16

In the country 18

On holiday 20

What's safe and what's not? 22

Glossary 24

Index 24

Going out

Going out is fun. You could be going out to the shops or to the park to play.

It is good to go outside for some exercise and fresh air.

Always go out with people
you know. Never go out
alone, even to the local shops
or to walk the dog.

Stay with your family or friends when you go out.

At the shops

If you are in a busy street, supermarket or shopping centre, stay close to the people you are with.

Hold hands with your Mum and Dad so that you don't get separated.

If you get lost, go into a shop and ask a sales assistant to help you phone your Mum or Dad. If you have a mobile phone, call your parents or carer.

Never speak to a stranger or accept a lift from someone you don't know.

Let's play

Playing outdoors is good for you.
Make sure an adult knows where
you are playing and who you are with.

Always sit on the swings, don't stand or kneel.

If you are playing with friends, stay with the group. Make sure you go home with one of your friends.

It is exciting to fly a kite on a windy day, but don't run off on your own.

At the park

Never play football or other ball games on the street. Find your nearest park and go there to play.

Always go to the park with your family or friends.

A pond can be very deep, so
be careful if you are feeding
the ducks.

Don't play or
run too near
the edge of
a pond.

The playground

At the playground you can play on swings and roundabouts. If you are playing on the climbing frame or the slide, do not push other children off.

On the slide, always go down feet first.

Be careful not to stand too close
to moving swings as they might
hit you.

Hold on tight when you are on the swings.

School time

If you walk to school, always make sure you go with someone you know. If the evenings are dark, wear something reflective on the way home.

These girls have reflective stripes on their bags. The stripes shine when it is dark.

After school, never leave with a stranger, even if they say your parents sent them. If this happens, tell a teacher straight away.

Stay in the school playground until your parent or carer comes to collect you.

Train safety

Never play on or near a railway line or railway crossing. Wait until the barrier is up and the light is green before you cross, even if you cannot see a train.

If you are waiting for a train, stand back from the edge of the platform. Let people get off the train first before you get on.

Never lean out of a train window while the train is moving.

Stand back from the edge of the platform until the train has stopped and everyone has got off.

In the country

It is best to wear trainers or boots when you are walking in the country. Strong shoes will stop you from slipping if it is wet and muddy.

If you are out for the day, take rubbish home with you or put it in a bin.

Stay on the paths when you walk in the country.

Look at, but don't touch, insects or wild flowers. Insects might bite or sting. Do not pick and eat berries or mushrooms. They could be poisonous and make you sick.

Butterflies love nettles. But do not touch — nettles give you a nasty sting.

On holiday

Going to the seaside is great fun.
Always tell an adult if you want
to swim or play in the water.

**Put on lots
of sunblock
when it is hot,
even if it
is cloudy.**

If you go camping, never wander away from the tent by yourself. Do not talk to strangers unless you tell an adult you know first.

If you have a campfire, sit well back from the flames or you could get burnt.

What's safe and what's not?

Match the pictures to the sentences to find out what's safe and what's not when you are out and about. Answers on page 24.

1. Be careful if you are near a pond – the water could be deep.

2. Don't pick wild flowers or touch nettles – they can give you a nasty sting.

3. If you get lost, use your mobile to phone your parents or a carer.

4. At the playground be careful on the slides, climbing frames and the swings.

5. Stay with your friends when you go out to play.

6. If you have a campfire, sit well back from the flames.

Glossary

barrier   a gate or long pole that is raised and lowered to stop people crossing. It is lowered when there is a train coming and raised when it is safe to cross.

nettle   a wild plant that has a nasty sting

platform   where you stand at the station while you are waiting for a train

poisonous   something that can make you very ill if you eat it

reflective clothing   clothing that shines in the dark so that people can see you

stranger   someone you don't know

sunblock   a cream that stops the sun from burning your skin

Index

berries 19

camping 21
climbing frame 12

evening 14
exercise 4

football 10
friends 5, 9, 10

insects 19

mobile phone 7
mushrooms 19

park 4, 10-11
platform (train) 17
playground 12-13, 15
pond 11

railway crossing 16
reflective clothing 14
roundabout 12

seaside 20
shops 4, 6-7
slide 12
stranger 7, 15, 21
sunblock 20
swings 8, 12, 13

train barrier 16
train windows 17

wild flowers 19

Answers to puzzle: 1c, 2a, 3d, 4e, 5b, 6f